DATE DUE

Demco, Inc. 38-293

The
Little
Bat
ainer

The Little Bat Trainer

Gwen Ebert

FOUR WAY BOOKS
NEW YORK

Editorial Office
Four Way Books
PO Box 535, Village Station
New York, NY 10014
www.fourwaybooks.com

Library of Congress
Catalog Card Number: 2001 132485

ISBN 1-884800-44-0

Book Design: Brunel
Cover Art: *The Little Bat Trainer* by Kathryn Borland

This book is manufactured in the United States of America and printed on acid-free paper.

Four Way Books is a division of Friends of Writers, Inc., a Vermont-based not-for-profit organization. We are grateful for the assistance we receive from individual donors and private foundations.

Funding for the 2000 Intro Series Prize in Poetry was funded in part by a generous donation in memory of John J. Wilson.

ACKNOWLEDGMENTS

These poems, some in different versions, first appeared in the following publications:

Alligator Juniper	Creation Story
	Sandhill Cranes over St. Michael's
Bellingham Review	This Lie, This Dark Man, This Mother
Blue Mesa Review	At the Turn of the Creek
CALYX Journal	Burden of Words
Kalliope	To the Clear Ditch
New Letters	Skin
Passages North	Yard Song
The Pittsburgh Post Gazette	Pulling a stem from the baby's mouth
Southern Poetry Review	American Insomnia
	David's Love for Jonathan
	Early Morning Train through Indiana
	Night Recess, Coal Street
Zone Three	Three Points Hill
The Twig Songs (chapbook)	Loin
Parallel Press, 2000	Montana Meadow Lark
	The little bat trainer
	Day of Gracious
	The Quavery Line
	Of You I
	Albuquerque, Christmas Eve
	What Love Does
	Night Recess, Coal Street

I want to acknowledge the invaluable support of friends, near and far, whose kind attentions have furthered my work. I am hoping you know who you are. As for astute and generous editorial assistance, I am indebted to a number of people. For giving the book its final form: Jan Beatty, Nancy Krygowski, Sharon McDermott, and Jennifer Lee. For insightful commentary: Barbara Edelman, Toi Derricotte, Ed Ochester, and especially Marilyn Annucci, who saw these poems through many incarnations. I am deeply grateful to my parents and family—for being there, always; to friends at the Community House in Pittsburgh—for believing in my work; and to Erica Magnus, for her sagacious humor and love. Finally, a big thank you to Lynn Emanuel for making this book possible.

To all my dear ones

~

As you circle and rest,
as you find a good dry spot
under the windowsill of the world.

CONTENTS

The Church Bell from Our Lady

1

2

3

The Church Bell from Our Lady

It rings three times   darkness to morning.
The crickets go on as the sky loses its cave.
I go on gaining courage like the rooster.
O voice before light,
I want to be out like an animal.
Hear the whistle for the roaming dog.
Once I was big as the ocean.
I want all those rivers back.
I want the bell in me.
I want my own storm.
I am some green country and a road.
I am the music I will marry.
I am a woman and a woman with child.
I am green, I am silent.
In the morning you cannot find me.
My hands are in poems like a bear in water.
My body wades a current you cannot see.
You hear the church bell ringing three times.
You hear the rooster, the crickets fade.
You don't know what is coming.

1

Loin

Beautiful old biblical word
for the groan between my hips,
the lonely lapping on shores.
Of the loins, a child, a fruit,
a bringing forth,
a sweet kind of crying. Loin.
Contain the silent
range of mountains,
snow melt at flood stage,
scent through willows,
rush of uncontrolled
and downward. Loin.
The slope, the horizon
giving way. Loin.
The depth between stars,
blue-black, maroon, that sound
in the word—an elk call
in the haze of frost. Life calling
life. Ancestry backward,
loin to loin. Pain
of childbirth. Pain
of no birth, loin.
The cloth over hair
and animal bell.
The ringing.
The monastery. Raw,
rain blackened trees
of the loin,
loin.

Montana Meadow Lark

What's this scrap of birdsong
in the memory?—

My grandmother Olive stands
in black and white prairie grass,
thin once, her arms contented.
Plain skirt, plain blouse.
A smile with a loose fit.
Water running in the draw.
She could have stayed.
Montana cowboys wanted her
at home—good cook from Milwaukee,
good farmer's stock.

My mother, nineteen in Glacier Park,
hikes from her wait shift in the lodge.
Feet ache. She still takes a trail
with a waterfall to herself.
She forgets a woman's clammering
to try harder, to be enough.
Wind blows it off in all directions.

Ten years later
we come along to see bighorn sheep
from the station wagon.
Later we're stuck in the gumbo road to Haver.
We meet a cousin once removed,
a brown skinned stranger
named after grandma.
She takes us
to the coolhouse in the hill.
Olive. Miles of it.
Snake tracks in sand.
She paints oil color buttes
and pronghorns.
Cooks three meals a day
for a table full of men
without words.

I remember this: eggs
and steak and pancakes
every morning.

When mom was young
she took a summer trip to the ranch.
Her mother had her change of life
there on the train
and bled in a torrent to Helena.
Tore her skirts into clot rags.
And those other story details:
an uncle whose heart stopped,
forking hay, and my mother—
breakneck over forty miles of dirt
with his body on the back seat.

Facts that stick like cheat grass.
I'm along some road in Idaho,
picking sage,
letting the empty
be familiar,
letting the wind
bring up a sweet nothingness.

A Load of Blue

He comes over when he's out of milk. We live in a compound:
four houses, an orchard, my goats, two dogs, one dirt driveway
between us. He parks his pickup in the back of my house and
forgets to shut the door. The cab is full of fast food discards,
contracts, clip board, pipe wrench, pair of sandals, bees on the
Miller can rim. Sometimes his back hurts from laying bricks.
It's so easy to pull down his sweats. No jock strap. Sometimes
I go to his house and step over jigsaws, the orange cord, the
dusty can of arrowheads, to find the part of him that isn't tanned.
Maybe it's the desert. It's hard to say where things begin or end,
indoors, outdoors, neighbor, lover, your dog, mine. Bugs walk
under the door at night. A lizard on the wall over the sink means
luck. Goats push open the screen to graze on house plants. Maybe
he'll hang that medicine cabinet one of these days. For now
it's in the truck bed, mirror side up: rough arms of cottonwood
carry a load of blue.

The women from Shiprock told me

Watch out at night,
walking by yourself—
Skinwalkers.
And don't whistle like that.
Spirits will come to you.

    In the parking lot
    a little black cur
    came out of darkness
    matted and limping.
    It quivered when I faced it,
    followed me
    like my own crippled spirit.
    I wanted to rescue

    the boy
    who was angry at me
    for keeping him
    from rock climbing.
    It was rainy, slick.
    Later, no ropes,
    he climbed anyway.

    Where he went
    the canyon split the earth
    like a skull
    fractured.
    Funeral done,
    nothing to speak of.

These things happen
they told me
all the time.
Suicides.

A drunk kid.
Be careful.
They seem
like nothing.

The Bright Verbena

A little cumulus cloud this morning.
Between the legs I'm ready to rain
desire at your touch or the least expression
of sunflowers leaning in the heat.
I can't walk out. The forest,
even in shadow, is too hot.

That crow's throat breaks silence again.
In the bottom of the sun-split arroyo,
rocks imprinted by the dead mollusk and coral
could, any minute, call on the sea
booming in my body's cove.

The stones would steam and the old kelp
quiver to life. The green hands of anemone,
the aching fish, and slowly,
the sunblind shark
would feel the true weight of water
and gleam in the darkness
and cut back through it again for you.

Black Oaks

I go back to three black oaks living across the road on the edge of the field. I loved them exactly like old maternal friends. Once, Frau van Neumann took my hand and held it to her bosom, not breast. She was foreign and unashamed to warm me there, let me see her huge horrible freckles. What I mean by trees—they were their own peculiar place. I felt their girth by climbing. I knew their twists and bulges, sensed their roots going down as far as their trunks went into air. I knew what it was to be with those roots. A painter once said, "Trees . . . what else is there?" meaning, light on limbs and splintered negative space. I remember fullness of form like a torso, the places to grip between ridges of bark. Old branches curled in gestures I memorized in ice glaze, in sharp relief of snow, bad November gloom. If I drew one you would know: fifty feet, rough black, dead limbs, hollows. I would make you see there is a heart somehow—a way of being with a child, the sympathy you find in a mammal's eye. I couldn't admit this to anyone. My sister laughed, and my father groaned when I stood at the window and sobbed to the sound of the ordinary progress of chain saws.

The little bat trainer

wakes at odd hours,
wearing his old baggies,
head in a muffle.

He brings his glowing jar,
the weighted socks. Sprigs
of soaked grass in his shoes.
The world is turning over.
Night side leaves a cool breath.

This he loves:
barely the light and limbs
bare, color of no color.
Fog dampened hair.

If the bats return
all swung-down, half-winged,
singing the music that no one hears,

then by stars
he will toss them the sock weight.
As they drop to dive for him
in their blindness,

no one imagines
the faces.

Sandhill Cranes over St. Michael's

Light from the open doorway glints on the chalice.
Scent of chili drifts from Montano Road.

The cantor sings with the voice of a crane
quavering and lost to the altitude.

The *Prayers of the People* trail
like long legs of birds along a brown river.

No one can follow a pure thought
while the sandhills flock overhead.

We sing, we kneel, we take the broken bread
like a burro grazing goatweed in the yard.

Faith is a habit, a sense at our backs, an instinct
to turn toward rippling clay—see the kestril,

the sparrow hawk, a quick swoop of shadow.
If we could, we would cross ourselves like that,

like something unexpected:
cloud burst, dust devil, flock of cranes.

Skin

On mountain slopes the sun hallucinates
on some blue flower. My skin, the fox,
sleeps in the open innocence of light.

Years later, I harvest the damage in my face.
Chemo-cream rakes mud around the lips,
scalds the crowfeet,
cuts fire trenches down from the nose.
Pardon the faint hawks burned in the forehead,
the old rip of skin like summer earth.

My dear endangered atmosphere,
you leave the century stripped and bewildered.
Did we mean for this bright cruelty?
Did we think of frogs on jungle stems,
peepers in mucky reeds across the North?
Scientists in dripping waders count amphibians.
Count again. From every backwater
they disappear.
Some trick of ultraviolet light
now enters the glistening pervious skin.

Useless egg strands float.
Black heart, black heart, black heart
I am sorry.

When I was six
I dropped the jar of pond water;
a tadpole squirmed in splintered glass.
So much lost at once:
doubling cells, bloom of the tail,
the small mouth feeding in fine green hair.
Budding legs and finger webs,
the water body comes to air,
to the slick sexual back
and eyes. Jewels on brackish waters.

I am writing this for our skin—
close as it gets—
our delicate membrane,
our thin guardian of the slippery unknown.
There's no hard evidence against this reckless age.
No holes in the sky to point to.
Just a mottling
above the left brow,
a murky and permanent absence
in the earth's watering eye.

One Side of the World

The creatures
who watch us
with amused love
are dying.

Sometimes, we
have nothing
to do with it.

Cicada,
the little Christ
hummed the
drone note
high in sooty towers.

Now its body
lies broken
on a step.
Lifted,
the wings
detach,
thorax drops
like an airy plumb.

We live,
it seems,
on a one-sided
world—

one tired

as a body
on the city bus
at night,

falling into itself,

head bent
in the wrong
direction.

When Talk Sways

My grandmother's vision is going
from a blank spot in the middle retina outward.
She sees a woolly hole, believes
in phone poles as trees.
I offer her true descriptions.
That is a vegetable stand.
Those are pumpkins, not tomatoes.
I leave out the rented camel giving rides near
the corn stalks dressed as ghosts.

If we drive toward light her eyes shrink
like tide pool anemone. Back and forth
she feels the sway of talk. Her son,
the pharmacist, pushes beta carotene,
the A's the E's. She says, *That's what I get*
for looking the sun in the eye.

In the restaurant light is low.
When I face her she looks pleased
around the edges.
Dead center, though, I see the place
where I am not.
It wobbles like the call
of geese lifting in the dark.

To the Clear Ditch

Now I leave the country of my skull.
I have no thoughts other than my body.
The teachings shelved in my shoulders
make me heavy, going down.
They say I am falling
like a fish from a water cage.
They say I will be lost:
everything silver, red flesh behind the gill.
Look to the black water.
Imagine my last shape.

Once I took a cross and carved a vagina into it
and wrapped it in bailing wire and buried it on a mountain.
Once I loved a god made especially for serfs and laborers.
He and his angels of shame inhabited me, the way gods do,
without thinking.

The goats in Lebanon climb into trees
to eat the leaves and graze on bark and air.
If I open my throat I will make the sound of an animal.
I want to sleep in rain all night and wake up shaking.
Wake up with hunger as my first song and thirst my second,
then my deliberate joy.

The earth is worn down in places.
Cottonwood leaves tarnish like old brass in the ditches.
Layers of mud, miracle of water, muskrat and mallard.
I tell the earth, *Take over.*
I tell my tired contritions, *Go
with creek silt, pyrite and sand.*

Mary, Sweet Stranger, What Do You Think?

1

We went to my one room cabin.
She held me near the woodstove.
Brilliant pine trunk through the window.
How stiff I was, hands frozen at my sides.
Dog tail thumped against the porch.
I tried not to believe this. I tried not to tell
myself my body loved hers.
In the morning I couldn't move.
Guilt lay on my chest like a god.
I told no one. I washed. I tried
not to let this happen again,
every few weeks.

2

His golden retriever with the
eager bandanna, the smell
of cedar fire and warm clay.
His arc in the jeans,
the overstuffed chair.
We rolled around with everything on.
Nothing premarital.
He asked why. Something,
I said, about religion.

We went to see O'Keeffe's exhibit.
Abiquiu cliffs and rose light,
a blue green slit.
Down the middle: a river,
a canyon, some natural opening.
I felt myself pool.

He asked if
I like the art. I said
it's not what I expected.

3

I tried to nanny with
husband and wife.
A baby to hold.
Back room life. At night
she knocked on the screen.
I let her in, I let her out.
The kiss and hush house.
She was gone in the morning.
God was on the chest.
A look in the eyes of the wife,
of the husband. A look
I could do nothing about.

4

I went to live in the dying
religious community.
Kept a roommate
who slept with men.
I tended goats.
In the chapel at night,
a pinon fire in a white cave.
Two candles. Windows dark:

Mary, sweet stranger,
mother of god, santos
of wood—
what do you think?

5

He lived next door.
I went over nights
for *One Last Try.*
He said, *Ok,* like a buddy.
Like a science experiment.
A neighbor. He fixed
my goat pen when it needed it.
I figured god must be tired:
the lesser of two evils,
and besides,
nice butt, nice hair.

I'm not kidding:
My four siblings married
each as virgins
and produced
a quiver full of arrows.
They had plenty
to talk about.
I was good and quiet,
your maiden aunt.

6

The last time I nannied
I cursed babies,
a twin at every tit,
the diapers in hot sun.
Tiny moths flew in at night,
scribbled irritating words
in the hair
on my skin.
I hated the desert,
the hoax of the dry.

7

Old friend and I used to pray
in the dark like sisters.
In a letter, she offered to pay
for my change of heart.
A weekend retreat.
The work of the Spirit
would set me straight.
I knew she was trying
not to kiss her girlfriend
deeply. I knew
she wanted to be
a good wife.

8

One night I dreamt
of a woman with long black hair.
I noticed she was God.
Tall and ordinary,
she leaned
clean as a black horse
under cottonwoods at night,
a summer wind, her kiss
like a wood boat
taking me
to waters I had lost.
I woke up tall and ordinary—
God, not a critical thing
in the world
left to guide me.

2

Day of Gracious

Now is a green and black
    day of gracious rain.
        The night of it left windows down
on the pale blue Pontiac.
    Ponds pooled in the foot wells.
        Beaded water broke and ran
down webs of sleep. Flashes
    and distant tombs, quart jugs,
        breakers, coal tumbling dreams.
Now the light comes full of sound.
    Birds courting in the rain   call
        cross warble from roof pitch
to alley shrub. Leaves
    unravel in the thrumming,
        as toddling hands
in the spout. The worked world is sodden
    while oblivion labors.
        And you sleep on
in a green and black time,
    because rain loves your body
        more than your mind,
because it hushes the hundred yard blowers,
    mowers, motors of the heart.

Early Morning Train through Indiana

I doubt they were strangers, sharing the train seat and passing talk
back and forth. I think the man in the striped tee and fatigues was
Mennonite, the giant with the blond bowl-cut was Amish—blue
sleeves rolled up. Both wore black boots spattered with manure. I
heard their words as I dozed in the darkened car: eggplant, turnips,
harvest, per bushel. I don't know where they had been, or why they
had traveled in work clothes from Philadelphia to Chicago. I don't
know who loved a long-skirted woman, or what was permissible, or
if either would give up their home acres, or if they ever wanted to.
I don't know what they dreamed.

I do know that when they spoke I heard an innocence: *Here we go,*
when the train started up; *chigachigachiga,* at the stop in Ohio; *Let's
go swimming,* when we reached the harbor. I do know that the sun
came up, that the landscape was ugly, that they studied it through
the window for its use and for abandoned machines. I do know that
work had made them beautiful—their faces and chests—and all
night across the aisle I wanted the Amish one's arms, as he cradled
his head, as he draped them across his woolen thigh.

Three Points Hill

Sun gleams on the orchard rise,
rows of black trunk,
knots of shriveled fruit.
Across the glazed snow
cows slip.
Hooves click and scrape
on blunt edged furrows.
They balance a heaviness,
breathe pale clouds.
Steam rises from the sudden
rush of hot piss.
Across the road the Pentecostal church
trails a bell rope—an ice snake
halfway through the door.
Light falls on crooked pews,
the cracking shades, the flag.
In seasons, blue and black mildew
grow across the song book
just as it was left
alone, alone, alone
with Jesus.

David's Love for Jonathan

I was the the stone embedded in Goliath's forehead. I was the Centurion's gorgeous boot. I was the scent of the whore's hair draped on Jesus' feet. I was Aaron's budding staff. I was the tar and bulrush basket, Bathsheba's towel, Delilah's shears, the jawbone of an ass. I was Samson's pillars pulling down. I was Abednego's furnace, the pit of lions. The pile of pot shards, Job's boils, King Saul's cut robe in the cave, David's lonely psaltery by night. I was the stench in the ark, the branch that hung Absalom, the brimstone begging Lot's wife to look back. I was Hagar's belly and Sarah's laugh at God, Mount Horeb trembling with the Law. I was the rock Moses struck in a rage, the murmuring over manna, the earring melted to make the calf. I was the bullock waiting to burn for Baal. I was the raven who fed Elisha, the goat snagged to stay the knife from Isaac, the burro who spoke to Balaam. I was a sheaf of Joseph's dreamy grain, the pit his brothers threw him in. I was the bottomless vial of oil, the visions in the scroll. I was David's love for Jonathan. I was the wall of parted water beginning to fall. I was Esau the hairy son, smelling of game, losing the birthright. I was honey and locust. The beam in the eye. The head on the platter, the handwriting on the wall. I was the scourge, the tables turned, the withered fig tree, the eye salve of spit and mud. The man who saw people like trees, the woman who touched the robe without asking. The hoard of demons sent out into swine, the herd rushing off the cliff, healed lepers who never came back, road to Emmaus, kiss in the garden, crown of thorns, scar in the side, tongues of flame, water to wine, ghost on the sea, seven stars and seven lamps of gold.

Grosstanten

The great-aunts, in their late-life maidenhood,
came to us like the Kings at Christmas,
with canisters of Lebkuchen, Springerling, Pfeffernusse.

Lydia turned red on Rhine wine.
After brandy they laughed from their bellies like men.
They got Grandma and Florence going—deep *har hars*.
Put their arthritic legs up on foot stools,
stretched them out straight as timber from the Black Forest.
Big shoes, orthopedic. Cube heels shining.

They wore dazzle earrings and scarf pins
on tailored suits from past office jobs
my father never talked about.
They were not wives.
What to make of widows, spinsters,
women who appeared at holidays
gut-chuckling, telling stories,
making comments in their own language.

Elsie once had Ed, the dead minister.
Louise had Arthur at forty, another one,
whose miniature German Bible
took up a tiny square of wood on a pedestal
in her living room. When we were good
we could open it and read the script
with a hand lens, like one of the Wonders
of the World, like the Lord's Prayer
inscribed on the head of a pin.

Lydia was true spinster—no holy ghosts.
Good for making jokes. Taught us to say,
You are a little dumbhead,
Du bist ein kleiner Dummkopf.
Gave us exotic wind-up toys,

hard-bound books beyond us,
hand painted eggs, ornaments,
the candle-lit glockenspiel—
cling, cling, cling, cling.

We would sing "Behold, a Branch is Growing,"
Es ist ein Ros entsprungen.
> and bears one little flower
> In midst of coldest winter,
> At deepest midnight hour.

My father made us stand to say
our scripture recitations, sing our hymns from school.
The Tanten recited the whole of Luke, chapter two,
in High Deutsch.
. . . and the angels said unto them, Fear Not.

And they did not,
as we did, fear our father.
They called him Jimmy,
and lived without men,
with each other in the city.
It was a marvel to us.

We opened their gifts of mukluks and knitted mitts,
small paintings of Chicory and Bloodroot.
These things took proper time, which they had
in a house with dark wood tables, spindly chairs.
Tick, tick, a cuckoo came out from a country,
on the hour, as expected.
We were still surprised.

This Lie, This Dark Man, This Mother

This crow heaving its shoulders to speak.
    This lie, this dark man, this secret holding
          still   while the landscape buckles
    and heaves under me.
            My dreaming steepens
                and steepens. Where are the stairs, is
                    my balance?
This lie, this dark man, this mother
    in the night
            while my sister
    slept, this creeping made me,
           made me, my body (a long time ago)
unlearn
its flower by flowering
          under some strange,   under part of the mind
                    falling away.   Where

    it didn't matter (a long time ago)   But where

is that rage and that secret? Now,   I want something
                 I can stalk, could mark, take
             in my mouth
                    whole
          and bite   real
         while I
               fall and fall and fall.

My lover kisses the folds where I   will not bloom for touch.
    No. Lust
             is too civil, is too rough, is too much scent
    in the daylight, not
               in my body's deep pocket.
              Alone,
I see myself in the mirror: my fungal fruit,
    my cauliflower, my little pet.

You—so small, and what you want, so plain,
and when, by going backwards
into old old rhythms of falling,
you do fall
but look. I am here
to study you, my little
doorway where a drapery shines
and you are nothing
but a kiss,
my sweet, my simple, my so simple.

No one else is here. No one stands all night in the closet. No one
knocks on the dream door quietly.
    I don't know who it is

                        (a long time ago)

who
      recognized my blooming under

                some   unconscious desire

Who   forgot   I was there,

            I would show

        the beast horn—fear.

I think
the bough did break.
I think the baby did fall   very
    badly
in love with the blind eye turned,
the pretty smile, the
nothing happened

the blind eye turned,
the pretty smile, the
nothing happened

very badly
in love with
the story

of no story

Nothing   of my own   keeps happening.

Pulling a stem from the baby's mouth

I tug gently, a leaf follows
gutter black,
wet from her gums.
The startled expression
passes like finch shadows
across brick.
Crows calling
and winter sunlight
stop her crying.
She sits wobbly on the
pavement, bare calves.
Touches pebbles
raised in the cement.
Hand falls to wet leaves.
Back to pebbles.
Cat ears twitch behind
the shrub. "Oh,"
she inhales a sound,
"Touch that!"
Black tail. Other.
She reaches and sees
her shadow hand.
Blue light and trees.
Everything
gets in her mouth.

Burden of Words

My sisters can barely finish a sentence. I watch them fish in the dark reservoir for a word bold enough to take on air. Water rumples from too much wind: father, grandfather, ministers in storm, ghosts of angry immigrants swinging their tools, teaching the fields to comply. I hear the ax ring somewhere in heart wood. In the far corners of the serf fields my great-grandmothers learn to work a harvest they will never keep. I am like them, women with thick waists, tired hands and a taste for pickled meats. One sits on a stool, plucking a goose. Her brows and mouth are full of feathers. The ax rings. Words fall. The silence around them is heavy as a cross, or the molecule which will carry it down the blood line. It is heavy as a fist on the pulpit. Heavy as God must be, taken ounce for ounce, verse by verse. *I know that in me, that is, in my flesh, dwelleth no good thing.* I try to make a good thing of words, work keeping the kitchen counters clean. I am like my sisters. Swipe the stone colored rag along the sideboard. Listen. Work is listening, watching, waiting, helping, bearing one another's burdens. Sometimes I would like a good burden to bear—not this hard collection of words, this heart wood, this center that was meant to give.

Of You I

Dreamed of you I
always had
a love for and
an appetite—

soul food you

We don't
in twenty years
but last night
dreaming
your face
came close

words
then breath
our lips
surprised by
what to do
taken by
our warm
old
obvious

A Woman in Old Growth

A tree like a woman stands
with one hand in her pocket
and one not knowing what to do.

Elephant skin of the ancient beech
is a back unaware of itself.

Rings of an old limb mound
like a breast.
Behind, the rough, red trunk
of a white pine rises
muscular in warm dry air.

Crickets drone
one fervent theme,
a descant riding

slowness of wind
and leaves
falling from high blue branches.

In old growth,
the hemlock's lace is a shadow
on the corpse of the standing dead.

I wish I could love my body.

A fine rigging glistens
in the jagged stump. Spider
on a little sea of moss. White
and hovering insects, full of captured light,
move up and down and nowhere.
A leaf falls on my page. A needle
in my hair.

It is easy to love the darkness
behind the leaves
of the seedling beech,
all veins in a bright green light.

These trunks at night,
some standing dead,
seem gods
with a few stars between them.
Trees full of holy silence,
impossibly close, bright,

leaning, towering
to return. Here,
I am wooden—
part hollow,
bark draped with webs
and seeds.

I don't know what to do with my hands,
but they want to move like leaves
over all the air
and at night, to fall singly
like a wild event.

The Quavery Line

A set of small, V-shaped twigs poking

through snow makes a sentence
written against grief. Though, to me,
it looks like hieroglyphs. Black mathematics

on white, a winter crop of bird feet.

When read from left to right, it could be
a musical score for the pulse
of a spider sleeping under bark,

or some unrecognized refrain

like the one I heard in my dream
during a bout of bleakness.
What a song. It had a rumba beat,

back-up band, chorus drifty as smoke.

The lead was hoarse and off key,
but my dream cast didn't care.
They sang along. And when I woke up

happy, I thought about V's, the linoleum V

made by my grandmother's legs as she sat
scribbling song lyrics between them
on the kitchen floor, kerchief bent for the radio,

while diapers filled, dishes soaked.

I call her sometimes when I need
something, but what? and she sings me
a '30s tune, says, "You know this one?"

Melodies, little rifts, twig songs in the snow.

At ninety, this is what her memory keeps.
This is what comes through, even in my sleep.
"You know this one?" she sings a quavery line.

No, I say, but keep going.

The Turtle

A woman who keeps her marriage for a piece of land (his), shows me a sandstone cliff near a swamp. I'm re-learning the names of trees. She knows everything, answers me with a wave in the rough direction of cherries, alders, white oak, black. The woman picks a crushed turtle from the road, examining its entrails and eggs. Shock of recognition: this is a Painted, the one we held two nights ago, alive. She had put it between us on the couch so we could study field guides, learn the orange design. Female, we decided. No dip to the underside. I hadn't seen this woman in a year. Bringing me a turtle was her way of saying she was glad I had come. Now she holds the web of shell-crush by a single claw. I don't want to look. She is small and tough around the mouth. She flings the wreckage into cat-tails—gesture like a shrug, gesture native to the rural working hard: *Here's something else you'd know if you knew anything.*

American Insomnia

There will be no dogs in heaven barking at night.
There will be no night, for which I am grateful,
and no sleep, which makes this moment almost heavenly.
It's a way of looking at things, say L.A.—or the empty car
being towed in the other lane and how lonely it is without the usual head
at the wheel. On airport escalators we seem so American,
looking at each other and looking for evidence of what we are
or should be. No one tells. No one claims their solo version
of humanity. No one invites the others in to rest on the beaten sofa.
We will not tease each other as if we were alike in embarrassing ways.
It's not a joking matter, the weight, the divorce, how we sit at the feet
of the television, asking over and over if this
is being alive, or is that, and will you play it for us again
in another set and wardrobe? Can we believe
the crowd of voices in the living room, bringing their drama and their cool?
Saturday night the saxophone crawls like a snake.
We can almost believe we are having a good time.
We can almost believe Talk Radio as a kind of neighborhood.
Pieces of family are left like derelict farm machinery in the stodgy states.
Our deli food comes ready made in takeout trays for one.
And one and one, everywhere, America in its choice, does not know
what to wear, when to laugh, how to love, how long.
Awkward as a digital clock—a money machine, angry as traffic
we are strung together by the high voltage buzz of our need.
It's on twenty-four hours a day, tireless as a glacier.
By strip malls and video stores it has eaten the landscape as a snack.
Now we cannot sleep. The old wilderness is gone
and a new one howls at night,
worse without predators and silence,
without mystery and soul—
more immense, more lonely, more inexhaustible.

3

Yard Song

My mother holds her famous wooden reel
while the clothesline unravels in rows,
a music staff on sky. She walks.
She loops the line, the handle squeaks.
Cardinals syncopate with crows.
Wood pins garble in the cloth sack.
Sheets are damp forms rounding—
slow crescendo of white.
My mother in her noon black halter top
makes a melody that starts as a thick soft rope
unraveling from wood
and ends at sea. Billow and sag.
All my life I have felt
the tension of flight from the rigging.
The nest of the oriole swings from
the elm. Sound I am lonely for
is my mother loosening
from a wrapped spindle,
her scent and motion
out on the line to drift and drum
while we played,
at anchor,
to gathering winds.

What Love Does

What love does begins in my body. Today, hours after the dance class floor, there is weariness in my arms. My thighs speak strangely all the way up the stairs. You stand in the lamp light with a beauty I will drink all evening, through my irritation, through my complaints, through my insistence that you do the dishes. My body drinks while my mind goes about her Martha duties. It is Mary who walks up to your face, Mary who kisses you several times, tenderly. My body's name, Mary. Physical—the moment, the lamp, the quilt, your skin, the scent of your neck and belly. I don't want to have you out of the old desire for wholeness. I want your presence, your tangle of curls, the amazing movement of your mouth as you speak something and I do not hear.

This is no secret

All we need is time.
April says they're smart
to give us two weeks off,
no more than that.
Too much time
can alter everything.
Every morning I take time.
Clouds shred.
Crickets accompany
towns out of darkness.
Time opens hands
like tree limbs to leaves.
Birds fall out.
In time I start to breathe.
I turn my neck on its stem
until the headache breaks.
I hear the little bones
at the base of my skull
clicking like cardinals
in tall trees.
Each bone takes
its natural space.
Each bird stakes
its own
territory of air.

The Scorpion at Dick's

Today I saw a real scorpion trapped
in the resin cast of a yo-yo on a rack
at the check out aisle, Dick's Sporting Goods.

How did the scorpion cross the road?
How many overturned rocks are there
in Mexico now? How many boxes of yo-yos

travel on highways to a national chain,
to hang with gummy bears and batteries?
The scorpion's market value is the way

it died imperfectly, tail bent—crackly,
translucent talisman of trouble.
And solidly, in a bubble of resin,

it's a symbol of what boys should like,
a creepy crawly thing to hold in the hand.
What does it look like when it spins—

walk the dog, cat's cradle—
when you play tricks
around the world?

Does it blur into a glassy eye with a ragged brown
pupil in the center? Does it watch, in the way
I hope that something watches

what is happening to us, how we have become
encased and spinning on the freeway
and back, on the freeway, back.

What good is the fishing rod or golf club?
There's a video that keeps playing in the camouflage aisle:
ducks in a marsh, a twelve minute sequence

repeating, in stereo staccato. I can't avoid
the worn out image, the patchy earth-tones
fading, while marked flocks rise up again

like grief in my chest. Never mind the dumbbells
I came here for, or the pecs and abs I wanted
to strain enough to feel.

I keep hoping for something
beyond my reach, beyond the cool air
blowing over the hoods of all this shining

and Chi Chi's, The Zip Lube, the back side
of the mall. Maybe someone forgot
to landscape a little ditch, and there's a rock there,

and underneath it, something is alive
and no one will have a clue
what to do with it.

Outside Like the Moon

What I remember is green sage
blowing over pink clay for miles,
horses running the flushed length of the sky.

The hair on my arms blew backwards.
That was all I thought.
Sheep between red mesas and gullies,
warm air and shadows.

There was nothing but wind.
I did not understand a thing.
I did not want to.
At night I prayed to my old Lord
to leave through the window
and stay outside like the moon,
to keep that kind of distance.

The Bad Guest

There's a piece of gristle lodged in my sleep.
Now the stench of a foreign cigarette in my bed,
in the fabric, on my fingers and papers. Hate
like a wedged fist of clay that will not flatten
into slab, or turn snakelike, or to a slick lump
spun on the wheel, spread under the thumb.
The dentist doesn't care about my mouth.
My tooth is is a headless woman wearing a dress
like a trampoline. There's a light and scope attached
to his eye. He spelunks in the molar's hollow roots,
the chambers of a little cave. I hear fine pointed crunching
deep in the mandible someone may handle, someday,
examine for its resemblance to a living thing.
This morning I feel strange all over, stiff
in every critical joint. Stupid, I tell myself.
Bones of my ass sick of the desk job,
of the stranger in my house who smokes without asking.
I hate his filterless smells, the bad cologne that follows
like an entourage. His mouth is mangled by disease.
I don't want to see that black striped suit. I'm tired
of my pity. I don't care why he smokes all night, shut up
in his room with a flask of instant coffee. He's just
on the other side of the wall. Light under the door. I smell
him. I know his ancient, monotheistic penis. The hairs
on my chin are sprouting stiff and black. Something
is eating away at my jaw, and shoulder joints and knees.
I'm gong to die with all of this self-hatred—bad guest
behind the door, the lit insomnious crack, the stink,
ashes dripping on the floor.

A House of Sorts

One morning she found herself on a clear blue plane
where all the other planes intersect.

This because of sex.
This because she wanted, finally,

to be angry, to be home.

There in the urban woods,
she forgave every green place

and the brown one, and the great lakes,
the steel belt with scars, the cities with car rivers,

this,

while she sat in a struck down tree.
Once high with thick branching,
it was now a curvacious tunnel,

a house of sorts,
with lots of shadow and dark,
light and air.

Dead as it was, all heaviness had
printed itself in the dirt.
No more wars with gravity.
Weeds went where they would.

And there she came to a place
for herself and her body,

a blue place and clear, the plane
and the many planes

which, coming together
all at once,

come together on the earth.

Holy Things

In the drawer of the nightstand
where my sister puts her blue cat glasses
I keep my little silver book
with Aunt Lydia's confirmation script
on the flap and a book mark attached,
the best part, silver ribbon with a metal
Holy Spirit dove dangling on the end.
This is *What Jesus Means to Me.*
Also, a bar of soap wrapped
in yellow sponge to look like a Bible,
sequin glued around on the cover,
a little plastic flower pinned through.
I don't know what to do with it.
On the shelf, a card with slits to fill
with dimes until it's heavy for Lent.
In the closet, on the light bulb chain,
a smooth white plastic cross
which glows in the dark and
fits perfectly in my hand
when I am looking for my shoes.

Night Recess, Coal Street

The School for the Deaf has a long lawn.
In the dark, after rain, it smells like lake water.
Deaf children play under yard lights.
Sound comforts:
from within their bodies
muffled hoots and warbles
travel great distances.
Who needs to understand?
Gestures conduct the orchestra of air.

Tonight, the air is full of towns
and lakes and things
I seldom say, or speak:
for instance, whom I love.
Through wrought iron fence
kids on a court are a silent film.
The ball itself seems to bounce
without sound.

These nights go against the rules.
Sensations murmur
in the palm, on the skin,
in the sway of heavy branches.
Dazzle of car lights, slickness of tire,
I am spying on a recess,
an absence of syllable.

I imagine words
I could live without.
Say, "lesbian,"
or "husband."
Watch language stake
its stupid claims.

Off the bus,
where I walk
by the School for the Deaf,
there is nothing
for me to understand.

The night is itself—
textures in wind,
a wild enthusiasm of arms.

Albuquerque, Christmas Eve

Yellow light through the paper luminario.
Yellow candles in our pockets.
In a yellow sheen robe, Brian
the dark-eyed priest remains
his Buddhist self
canting Episcopal prayers
in the brave lonely space above our heads.
Pagan poet Tim sits next to me by accident.
Our shoulders are old friends
bumping on the downbeat of *Angels*
We Have Heard. Angels, as I remember
are blue and earthen brown.
My relief is particular as stars in their black bowl.
The mountains here still sleep like dogs—
circle and rest, find a good dry spot
under the windowsill of the world.
Brian says,   *Who could really follow a star?*
                How many animal sheds were there
                in Bethlehem? Don't you think
                God was hard to find?
I used to hate this desert town. Thought it
my exile from something called home.
Colored it with every kind of sadness.
Now, it is simply yellow.
Some red, some brown. Green in the mountains.
Scrub green stippling the foothills.
Phyllis, in her green uniform, keeps
the trails I used to walk. In La Cienega
she was stalked by a cougar. Tells me
it was high in the rocks and growled down.
Elusive, but still around. We agree—
a good sign. Everything seems a sign:
the three extinct volcanoes and the broken
channels of the Rio Grande, the low-crouching
barber and pawn shops on Fourth Street.

In a backwards way
I'm always learning to love
what's here, to belong for good
to an innocent ground. Tonight,
I don't need a star to follow,
but I'll take the map that Phyllis made
of a trail I could walk in my sleep:
Mud Spring to the ridge, down Paradise Canyon.

Creation Story

And so we appeared in cactus flowers and soft green wind
with shining minds.

Our needs began as water and food,
an overhang of rock. A tool or two.

Some whittled and chipped their way out of rawness.
It wasn't luck.

Others made the signs of amazement
and departure: road beds, potsherds, lions made of stone,

language, coal mines, railroads.
Who could have dreamed such flight and weaponry,

systems, surgeries, screens? Now the whole of it is ours
and we are going fast on the interstate,

a place that doesn't feel like a place,
though hawks still live on the edge,

and we count them, bored by what we've made
like God, dreaming of the flood.

What's to be made of the bloated gut of deer
or the leafless irrelevance of trees?

What does it mean to have two legs, really,
and no one to greet, as on that fine, first day

when the flute call was wind scent and howl,
tracks at the stream, the world—our companion?

Yesterday, seven leaves floated fast down a curbside drainage:
a melody of color and motion. One of us wanted

to wave to them, she was so happy again,
so almost human.

At the Turn of the Creek

It was dusk after the cook-fire. At the turn of the creek I sat where water would flush towards me, clear. I was fed as if I were the pool at the turn. A beaver swam in slow circles. In my mind, Duane's voice told the stories over again, from the afterlife of the Sioux. How his dead father returned to him and stood behind the truck in the yard. Warned the family of trouble. How, living with Navajos now, he does not throw away the broken chair. Sometimes his mother's ghost comes down from the north, to sit there—to watch his children.

The water was turning gold under black banks with straw hair. Last night we camped on snow. I woke once, afraid of the cold and the dark bowl of the mountain. Everything was tactile and fierce. In my dreams I found a wood frame house. Room with sunlight, kids on a worn green rug. The stairwell with pictures of my German kin, people, my own, a thousand miles away. From that place of lakes and farms I want to tell him that I know. My grandmother comes to me sometimes, through her bread boards and bowls, and watches like the ghost of any Sioux.

The Watershed

Of all the keys she keeps, two are sacred.
One opens the hinged box of her jaw,
from which
a few small syllables escape
as the plain birds she learned
in childhood:
Never draw attention.
Try not to offend.
Be helpful.
Ask for little.
Also, she keeps there
a small stone of desire
to break jaws,
many jaws.

Take the other key.
It is beautiful from neglect
like the child's drawing of a lady:
her lashes sweep to the sky,
her nose,
the nose of a pig.
The key shines
like the watershed
of the Kickapoo
set aside to be dammed,
and then forgotten.
Creeks twine the hills
in shallow and bowls.
Womanly trunks
of trees left to time
sprawl
into dark fantastic forms,
roots that go
where they will.

Rite of Ravens

Here I sleep with mosquitoes
scribbling at my ears.
Here the bowl of the universe
spills, and fish feed on surface stars.

Here with my terror
of the rising delta flukes of whales,
I enter the realm of enormity—
mountains in mist—
cold hands gripping the paddle.
I fall into moss tangled,
thick and rotting fragrances,
into forgotten hallways
of the earth's heart.

Seals and snow peaks wake at dawn.
Here, in whistle tones, the eagle.
Here, in sick swells, my body
like a guilemot, a murre, a whip of bull kelp
torn from its black mooring.

I ride out from the eelgrass flats.
I ride out on the creature skin
of this slick lolling form
whose eyes appear in the startling
bloom of the jellyfish,
whose body roams beneath me,
muscle flesh of water.

Fierce matter, bearded shore,
I beach so often on your trembling stones.
I climb the towering drift wood
root mass of the dead.
Here I am rust colored—
a humming bird in alders,

a sea worm coiled
in a snail's white hollow.

I am the one drinking
the three spun notes of the hermit thrush.
I am the one with unbearable thirst for substance,
whose sorrow limps along the edges of the world.
I am the one who shelters
a withered and shrunken desire,
the one who halts at the lip
of your ceaseless break and foam, your roar.
I am the one whose grief is an absence,
who sleeps the little coma of despair.

A white sky stirs dark waves.
I see the wreckage of plastic and shattered crab.
I see the live and manifold limbs
of the sunflower star.
On the rain-shook path through Sitkas and firs,
feet tear through into serpentine caverns.
Three thousand years of sun and storm
tower and will fall,
will some
or all be taken.

Cambium, showers, blasts of wind and thrashing.
Mussels crush under foot.
Nothing is without voice or wanting.
I float and cannot feel the bottom
of this rocking, but there
in sword ferns on the shore,
—fierce eyes,
raven masks. Ghosts
of the last shell midden.
What ceremony brings the
hermit crab in various adornments?
Timber, stripped and littered from the barge,
gathers for a howling fire.

Down, and in small breaths
barnacles open their bodies
and gesture with fine haired
legs, or tongues, or words.

I bend to your lowest tide. I listen.
The wet sand spurts and speaks.
Wake me with all of your cool color
and cawing, trees like breaching whales,
and even dying, come to me
as bladder wrack and song.
Keep me in the ferocious shoals
of wanting—
you, other, strange
and smallest of crabs darting sideways.

Gwen Ebert lives and works in Madison, Wisconsin. The inspiration for some of the poems in this book is drawn from her experiences teaching outdoors in the Southwest. She is the author of a chapbook, *Twig Songs* (Parallel Press, 2000), and her poems have appeared in such publications as *New Letters, Passages North,* and *Kalliope.* She has been a recipient of *Southern Poetry Review*'s Guy Owen Prize, selected by Mary Oliver, *Heart Quarterly*'s first poetry award, and a 49th Parallel Prize from *The Bellingham Review.* She received her MFA from the University of Pittsburgh.